CHEROKEE

JUL 6 - 1990

Looking at Weather

Don Radford and Peter Radford

B.T. Batsford Limited   London

Typeset by Tek-Art Ltd, West Wickham, Kent
and printed in Great Britain by
Anchor Brendon Ltd,
Tiptree, Essex
for the publishers
B.T. Batsford Ltd,
4 Fitzhardinge Street
London W1H 0AH

ISBN 0 7134 5046 0

Contents

Acknowledgment

The Author and Publishers thank the following
for their kind permission to reproduce copyright
illustrations: Aerofilms Ltd, pages 10, 11, 29,
35, 44, 45; Associated Press Ltd, pages 17, 21,
28; Mr T. Bodford-Cousins, page 30; Camera
Press Ltd, page 8; Mr Allan Leas, pages 12, 25;
Mansell Collection Ltd, page 27; The
Meteorological Office, pages 16, 36 (Crown
Copyright), 37 (Crown Copyright), 38;
Popperfoto, pages 18, 20, 22, 23, 26, 33, 43;
University of Dundee (Electronics Laboratory),
page 15; Mr W.K. Young, page 6. The
illustrations were researched by Alexandra
Wiessler. The diagrams were drawn by Mr R.F.
Brien.

Introduction

Every day the TV screens and daily papers carry news about the weather. This popular topic of conversation affects us all. Tinker, Tailor, Soldier, Sailor, together with Dick, Tom and Harry are all concerned about the weather. It governs the success of garden fêtes and cricket matches; it is responsible for pile-ups on the motorways, the life and death of many wild animals and even the fate of nations. Floods, droughts, blizzards, fogs and fine, sunny weather govern our lives, even more surely than kings and tyrants. Too much rain and a country such as Bangladesh is a vast stretch of muddy water dotted with groups of wretched humanity. Too little rain and the famines of Africa remind us that we are not Lords of Creation. Throughout history some nations have risen high and have then been cut down by a change of weather. Four thousand years ago a great civilization of NW India crumbled and vanished because the seasonal rains of the monsoons failed to arrive. Changes in weather and climate have forced whole nations to migrate and move out of Asia, just like Adam and Eve being cast out of Eden.

Weather may be something of a joke to most of us in Britain, just a topic of conversation; but to some people it is a matter of life or death. It is therefore a subject of great importance and one that deserves to be studied and not casually dismissed.

In Britain our weather changes from day to day. We do not go to bed each night expecting that tomorrow will be the same as yesterday or yesterday fortnight. As far as we are concerned, variety is the spice of life and our weather, if nothing else, does provide us with variety. From day to day and month to month our weather changes:

> Snowy, Flowy, Blowy.
> Showery, Flowery, Bowery.
> Hoppy, Croppy, Droppy.
> Breezy, Sneezy, Freezy.
>
> (Geo. Ellis, "The Twelve Months")

Powering the Weather Machine

It is hard work pedalling up hill on a bicycle. You are using energy generated in your muscles to propel you along. All machines need energy to make them work. The energy generated in your muscles comes from chemical reactions in which the reactants are obtained from food and oxygen in the air. Your food comes from animals and plants and both of these depend upon sunlight. The Sun is the primary provider of the energy needed to make your food. It also powers the Weather Machine.

The Sun is a giant nuclear furnace and in nuclear reactions mass is changed into energy. Every second the Sun converts 657 million tonnes of hydrogen into 653 million tonnes of helium. The missing 4 million tonnes is radiated as energy. Some of this energy falls upon the Earth. What happens to it then is quite a complicated story.

First of all, on an average, 40% of the incoming energy is immediately reflected back into space. This reflection from clouds, water and the surface of the Earth is called the albedo of the Earth and changes from place to place. A snowfield reflects more energy than a ploughed field. Its albedo is higher than that of the soil.

The 60% that is absorbed (made use of) consists of heat rays, the visible spectrum (red, orange, yellow, green, blue, indigo, violet)* and ultraviolet rays. Green plants make use of the visible spectrum to build up sugars and starches, which are food for animal life. The heat rays are used to heat up the atmosphere and clouds; to change ice and snow into water and water into water vapour. They also warm the surface of the Earth.

If this were all that happened, the Earth would steadily heat up and become white-hot. There is another side to the coin. As well as heat being absorbed, there is also heat being radiated back into space. There is a balance: incoming energy equals the outgoing energy. If the two do not balance then, overall, the Earth becomes either hotter or colder, depending on which side of the balance is greater.

Most natural phenomena tend to adjust themselves until an equilibrium is set up. If the Sun's output of energy increased, then the Earth would become hotter. As the Earth became hotter it would radiate more energy, because the hotter a body becomes the more energy it radiates. Ultimately, at some higher temperature, a new balance would be set up.

Another thing happens to the heat, light and ultraviolet energy that is absorbed. Some of it is converted into energy having a longer wave-

*To help you remember the order of the colours in the spectrum, learn this sentence: Richard of York gave battle in vain.

length and is re-radiated. Much of this longer-wave-length energy is then absorbed by the water vapour and carbon dioxide in the atmosphere and leads to its heating. Such heating of the atmosphere is known as the "Greenhouse Effect" because the atmosphere acts like the panes of glass in a greenhouse, not allowing the longer waves to pass through it. It has been suggested that without the Greenhouse Effect the average temperature of the Earth's surface would be 25°C colder than it is. In other words, the Earth would be mostly a frozen, lifeless ball.

The energy story is by no means complete. The same amount of solar radiation is spread out over more and more land surface as we travel towards the poles. Putting it another way, the same surface area receives less and less energy as the latitude increases. Not only is there less energy per square metre, because of the geometry of the system, but also the Sun's rays have to pass through a larger amount of atmosphere and run the risk of being reflected off clouds or absorbed by the air. You can see the same effect on any sunny day. As the Sun sets, the path of the rays through the atmosphere becomes longer, and so the power of the Sun diminishes. Its light becomes redder because the other colours of the spectrum (V.I.B.Gr.) are absorbed to a greater extent than the Y.O.R.

It is the unequal heating of the Earth's air and surface that provides the driving force for the Weather Machine. If we compare our Weather Machine with a steam engine, then the hot tropical regions can be compared with the boiler and the cold polar regions with the steam engine's condenser. The boiler generates steam that drives the pistons and then is condensed in the condenser. The tropics generate masses of hot, moisture-laden air that drives the air circulation over the planet. Moisture-laden air cools as it moves northwards, precipitating rain as it goes. There we have a hot-air machine powered by the Sun.

Block diagram of a steam engine.

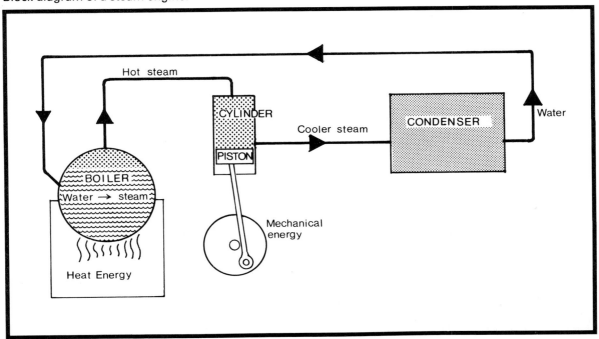

The Atmosphere

The air around us is so commonplace that we scarcely consider it. It is only when the winds blow, or we are aware of choking smoke and smog, that we take any account of the Earth's atmosphere. It was not until the seventeenth century that people we would call scientists began to study it. It all started with Galileo.

Galileo, who lived in Italy from 1564 until 1642, was one of the most famous scientists of his day. In 1638 he was asked to solve a problem. The engineers of an Italian nobleman, Cosimo de' Medici II, found that they could not build a suction pump capable of pumping water out of a 15-metre-deep well. Unfortunately, Galileo was blind and so he referred the problem to his brilliant pupil, Torricelli. In 1644 Torricelli put forward the idea that the pressure of the atmosphere is capable of supporting a column of water about 30 feet (9.14 m) high or a column of mercury of about 30 inches (761 mm). He also suggested that the atmosphere thins out as we climb a mountain. The French scientist and philosopher Blaise Pascal (1623-62), shown in the picture, thought of the atmosphere as being like a great mass of wool, 30-60 metres thick.

The bottom layers would be more tightly compressed than the layers at the top of the mass. Also, if a handful were taken from the lower layers it would expand. So, he argued, if a known volume of air at the bottom of a mountain were taken to the top of the mountain, then the air also would expand.

Thinking about this analogy, Pascal had a bright idea. The atmospheric pressure would drop as one climbed a mountain, and the atmospheric pressure could be measured using a Torricellian barometer. The difference between the pressure at the top and the pressure at the bottom of a mountain would be a measure of the height of the mountain.

Pascal could not test his ideas himself and so he asked his brother-in-law, Florin Périer, who lived in Clermont-Ferrand, to carry out an experiment for him. The Michelin guide for the Auvergne describes what happened:

> As he [Pascal] was in Paris, he asked his brother-in-law, Florin Périer, to carry out the experiment. He was to choose a fine day, and in the company of some of the Pères Minimes, was to climb the Puy de Dôme taking with him a barometer. To his delight he found that the height of the mercury on top of the mountain was 8.4 cm lower than it had been in Clermont.

(The Puy de Dôme is an ancient volcano, 1,465 metres high. The Pères Minimes were members of a religious order in Clermont.)

Soon after the idea of "atmospheric pressure" was accepted, people began to associate it with weather. It was noted that the barometer was low during stormy weather and high during fine weather. So the science of meteorology began.

The study of atmospheric pressure led to

Otto von Guericke's demonstration of the immense force that the atmosphere can exert. In 1654 in Magdeburg (now in East Germany) he carried out his famous experiment in which two teams of eight horses could not pull apart two hollow hemispheres placed together and from which the air had been pumped.

More experiments with air pressure led to the invention of the first mechanical steam engine by Thomas Newcomen in the early 1700s. Strictly speaking, this engine was an "atmospheric engine" because steam was used to create a vacuum under a piston. Then, when the steam condensed, air pressure drove the piston down. It was the air pressure which did the work, not steam pressure. Even James Watt's engines were powered largely by air pressure.

In 1783 the Montgolfier Brothers built the first man-carrying balloons. These large paper bags filled with hot air rose in the air until the weight of air displaced by the balloon just equalled the weight of the balloon and its load. Today hot air ballooning is a popular pastime and large rallies are held every year.

Balloons were used to study the atmosphere. Soon it was found that if the balloon flew too high, the occupants found it difficult to breathe. With increased height both the air temperature and the air pressure drop and, at the height at which modern jet-liners fly (30-40,000' or 10-13000 m), travellers would rapidly lose consciousness and suffer frostbite unless the cabin were both pressurized and heated.

Our ocean of air does not have a definite boundary as we go up and up. It slowly fades away.

The layers of the atmosphere.

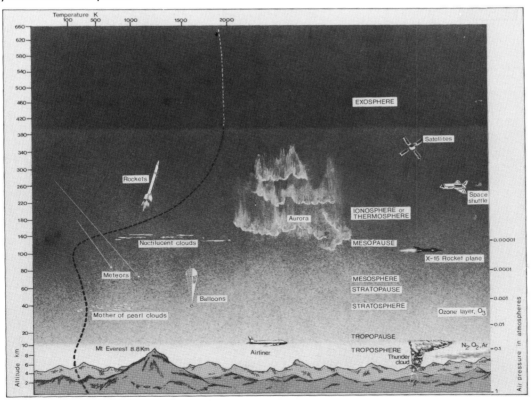

Clouds, High and Low

From out in space the Earth looks like a blue ball covered with large, ragged areas of white. These white areas are either clouds or snowfields which reflect back into space the rays of the Sun. On Earth most clouds are made up of tiny droplets of water, so small that they remain suspended in the air. Some clouds contain small ice crystals: the high-flying, fine, feathery Cirrus clouds are made up of ice particles usually formed directly from water vapour in the air. This process of changing directly from a gas to a solid without first forming a liquid is called sublimation. (The name is also given for the change, solid to a gas.) If you spend a few minutes looking at clouds you can see that they are continually changing. Sometimes, as with the large, cotton-wool clouds of summer, they seem to be boiling, as portions expand and rush upwards. Clouds like these are not just drifting across the sky. Inside

them air is rising rapidly; it is unstable. These clouds with their rapidly rising currents of air (up to 60 mph; 100 km/hr) are sought by glider pilots who can use them to gain height. Clouds with flat bases and swelling, domed tops are called Cumulus clouds.

Cumulus clouds, the cotton-wool clouds of a summer's day, are among the commonest clouds we see. They start life on the ground. Where you have a varied landscape some portions will warm up more quickly or hold heat longer than the surrounding areas. The air above these areas will also be heated by different amounts. Warmer air will tend to rise because when warmed, air expands and becomes less dense than colder air. This rising air or thermal is shaped like a doughnut. As the thermal (which contains water vapour as well as warm air) rises, the air expands and cools until, at a temperature called the dewpoint, droplets of water are condensed and a cloud appears.

A Cumulus cloud rises until it is in equilibrium with the air around it, that is, it neither rises nor falls. If enough clouds are formed they make a layer called a Stratiform cloud. If not enough clouds are formed then the ones that are produced slowly evaporate and disappear. So the Cumulus clouds are born, grow, reach old age and finally disappear. They often form long strings of clouds (left) as the wind gently blows them away from their point of origin.

Sometimes the Cumulus clouds grow and grow, fed by fiercely rising masses of hot air, until they reach 9-12,000 metres (30-40,000 feet). Then they form Cumulonimbus clouds, boiling cauldrons of energy. In these clouds electrical charges build up until, in a searing flash, lightning bolts stab down to earth. Hurricane winds within the cloud are so

powerful that they can tear to pieces any aircraft whose pilot is foolish enough to enter it. Violent up-and-down winds occur side by side, so that a plane can have, at the same time, one wing wrenched upwards and the other wing forced downwards. These are the savage forces that can tear to pieces even a powerful bomber aircraft.

The Cumulus cloud is like the geni in the bottle, sometimes small and gentle, but occasionally a monstrous brute. It is the Dr Jekyll and Mr Hyde of the natural world.

Stratus is a low-level, stratiform cloud. It is the typical cloud of November. It has a low cloud base, seldom above 500 metres (1500 feet) and is associated with fog and poor visibility. It spreads from one dim horizon to another, a thick grey sheet of gloom. An aeroplane flight after thousands of miles in brilliant sunshine can end by descending through several miles of swirling, obscuring layers of Stratus cloud to emerge from the cloud base close to the aerodrome.

There are other stratiform clouds, for example, the mackerel sky and the lens-shaped clouds that form in the lee of hills and mountains. These clouds indicate to glider pilots areas of rising air.

Both Cumulus and Stratus clouds are born and formed in the lower layers of the troposphere. In the upper troposphere are found the thin, feathery Cirrus clouds. The second photograph shows the conditions likely to be experienced by the pilot of an aircraft as it climbs to or descends from its operating height. Below lies an unbroken layer of Stratus clouds. Above are the Sun and high-level Cirrus clouds.

High in the sky between 60,000 and 100,000 feet (20-30 km) sometimes, after sunset, pinkish, irridescent, "mother-of-pearl" clouds can be seen. Because they are so high they can be seen from far away. On one occasion during the summer of 1984, clouds over the Scottish mountains were visible in Bath, 400 miles (650 km) to the south. On another occasion clouds above the Derbyshire Peak district were sighted 200 miles (325 km) away. Little is known about them except that they are most likely formed of ice crystals.

Very infrequently, after dark during the summer months, faint blue ripples of clouds appear in the dark bowl of night. These are 50-60 miles (80-97 km) high and seem to be made up of ice-coated grains of cosmic dust entering the lower atmosphere. They are called Noctilucent clouds and have been investigated by firing rocket probes into them to bring samples back to Earth.

Louise Young, in her book *Earth's Aura*, described clouds as being the "spindrift of the Ocean of Air", an accurate metaphor and description of things we see every day and of which we seldom take much notice.

Restless Oceans of Air

The oldest surviving Greek stories tell of the war with Troy and of the adventures of the hero Odysseus as he journeyed home. Odysseus was helped by Aeolus, "Warden of the Gales". Aeolus imprisoned the boisterous energies of all the winds in a leather bag, sealed it with silver wire and gave the bag to Odysseus. He commanded a westerly breeze to help Odysseus on his way. You can read all about the adventures of Odysseus in the Penguin classics book *The Odyssey*.

The air of the Earth's atmosphere is in perpetual turmoil; the winds hurry and scurry

here and there and yet, amidst the confusion, there is order. Winds blow because the air pressure in one place is lower than it is somewhere else. The direction of flow is from high pressure to low pressure and we can see from where the wind blows by looking at flags and weather vanes on the tops of buildings.

If we look at a global picture of winds we can see that there are patterns of flow. In our latitudes (50°-60°N) the predominant winds are those from the SW. The latitudes around 30° are known as the Horse latitudes, where sailing ships were sometimes becalmed for weeks. Farther south there is a belt of NE Trade Winds, the winds that blew sailing ships to the Caribbean. To the south of the NE Trades come the Doldrums, another region of calm or little wind existing just north and south of the Equator. It was here that the "Ancient Mariner" of S.T. Coleridge's poem was becalmed. South of the Equator come the SE Trades, the Horse latitudes and then the Roaring Forties, a belt of west or northwest winds between latitudes 40°S and 60°S. These winds howl round the Earth unhindered by land except that of South America; all the rest of the time they blow over the sea. This is why Cape Horn is such a fearsome place. There is nothing to stay the force of the wind. To complete the picture, from both the North and South Poles cold air flows to warmer regions.

In the regions 40° to 60°N and 40° to 60°S lies the battleground between cold polar air moving towards the Equator and warm, moist air moving towards the poles. These masses of air dance around each other and give rise to our own variable weather. More will be said of colliding masses of air over the page.

Wind was and still is the sailors' friend and foe. Too much wind and sailing ships lost their

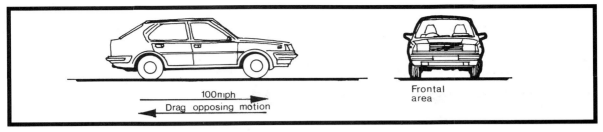

100mph
Drag opposing motion

Frontal area

Drag.

masts or were capsized; too little wind and ships lay becalmed sometimes for weeks. On dry land winds are just as deadly. Gales "raise the roofs" and blow down trees and even concrete cooling towers of electricity generating stations. The worst gale in recorded history was that on 26/27 November 1703. Daniel Defoe, the writer of *Robinson Crusoe*, who lived in London at the time, tells that twelve warships were wrecked on the Goodwin Sands, hundreds of ships were damaged in harbour, a hundred churches stripped of their lead roofs, 400 windmills blown down, 17,000 trees uprooted in Kent alone. And all because winds were blowing from high pressure to low pressure.

How is it that thin, insubstantial, airy-fairy stuff like air can act like a battering-ram and blow things down? To answer this question we have to turn to a branch of study called Aerodynamics – the study of air in motion. This is the science that is used when designing aeroplanes, bridges and modern motor-cars. Nowadays we hear that such and such a car has the lowest C_D of its class. This C_D is the "coefficient of drag" and is applied to aeroplanes as well as to cars. One thing must be made clear: the forces acting on a car or aeroplane moving at 100 mph in still air are just the same as if the car or aeroplane were standing still and air was blown over it at 100 mph. In both cases the drag force = 1/2 × (density of the air) × (air velocity)^2 × (front area of car or aeroplane) × C_D.

The density of the air is known at varying temperatures and pressures; the air velocity and the frontal area can be calculated; and the drag force is the same as the force that is needed to keep the aeroplane or car stationary. This can be measured in an aerodynamic laboratory. The only unknown is C_D and by putting the right figures in the equation, it can be calculated.

You will notice that the drag force is proportional to the square of the velocity. Suppose that at 3 mph the drag is 1 unit; then if you increase the speed from 3 mph (walking speed) to 96 mph (the top speed of a 1300 Metro) the drag force increases by a staggering 1,024 times.

The force of the wind was mostly an unknown factor to civil engineers before the Tay Bridge disaster of 1879. When designing and building this bridge the civil engineers had underestimated the wind pressure on the structure. This, coupled with flaws in the cast-iron pillars, led to the catastrophic failure of the main spans as a train was passing over the bridge one stormy December night. All on board the train were killed in the icy water of the Tay Estuary.

It is impossible to measure the effect of gale-force wind upon a full-size bridge or aeroplane, but scale models can be built and then tested in a Wind Tunnel.

Knowing the force of the wind, it is not surprising that it can carry dust and sand long distances. Saharan desert sand is regularly carried across the Atlantic on the wings of the NE Trade Winds. This dust gives rise to the wonderful sunsets in the Caribbean. In 1815 a volcano in the East Indies blew itself to pieces. Many cubic miles of rock was blown into the atmosphere in the form of fine dust. The results were catastrophic. 1816 has been described as the year without a summer. In England it rained every day, except for three, between March and October. It has been estimated that the average world temperature dropped by 3°C.

Fronts: Colliding Masses of Air

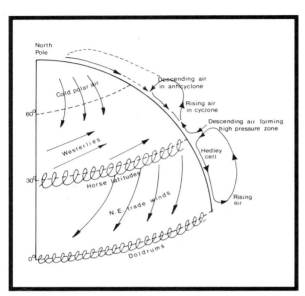

Movement of air in the Northern Hemisphere.

Our Weather Machine, powered by the Sun's energy at the Equator, moves vast volumes of air upwards and polewards. To replace the heated air, streams of ice-cold air from the poles flow towards the Equator. The stage is set for the battle of the Titans. First of all, the equatorial air rises and its place is taken by air brought in by the NE and SE Trade Winds. The hot equatorial air rises and moves polewards, sinking at about 30° latitude to form a subtropical high-pressure area. When air is compressed to form a high-pressure area it becomes warmer (just as the air in your bicycle pump becomes hotter when you blow up your bicycle tyres). Some of the air in the high-pressure area moves towards the Equator as the Trade Winds and some moves toward the pole. The region between latitude 30° and latitude 60° is the battleground of two adversaries, cold polar air and warm subtropical air, which wheel and charge at each other like two rugby scrums.

This area of conflict is called the Temperate Zone. Within it, countless systems of high- and low-pressure areas march endlessly round and round the globe. These systems produce our variety of weather – rain and drought, wild winters and scorching summers. In the winter, when the Sun is south of the Equator, the high-pressure systems move southwards and the cold polar air has the advantage. In the summer the reverse happens (we hope).

A high-pressure area is called an anticyclone and in summer it promises light winds, clear skies and warm weather. All this is due to the fact that as the air sinks its pressure rises and so does its temperature. With the exception of the cotton-wool clouds (Cumulus) formed by thermals, other clouds do not form very easily.

A cyclone, or low-pressure system, is a different kettle of fish. It is formed as the result of a battle between cold polar air and warm, moist subtropical air. These two adversaries do not readily mix. The boundary between them is quite sharp and on a weather map (synoptic

Weather map of a low-pressure system in the Northern Hemisphere.

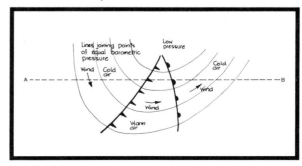

chart) the front is shown by a thick line with either triangles or half moons on it.

Looking down on a low-pressure system from space, we see it as a mass of clouds swirling round a centre that steadily marches towards the east. Satellites are constantly photographing the Earth and relaying the picture back to weather stations. The section across the depression (below) shows the distribution of clouds.

Generally, the cold front moves faster than the warm front and so there comes a time when the cold front undercuts the warm front and a part of the leading cold air. This is then called a Cold Occlusion. This undercutting cold air is colder than the cold air in advance of the warm front. Sometimes the overtaking air is not as cold as the cold air ahead of the warm front, and so it over-rides the colder air. This is called a Warm Occlusion.

Take another look at the weather map showing the circulation of winds round a low-pressure area in the Northern Hemisphere. The winds blow round and round the centre in an *anti*-clockwise direction. If you stand with your back to the wind, the low-pressure centre in the Northern Hemisphere will be to your left. In the Southern Hemisphere things behave in the opposite way. The winds blow round the low-pressure centre in a clockwise direction and, standing with your back to the wind, you will have the low-pressure centre on your right.

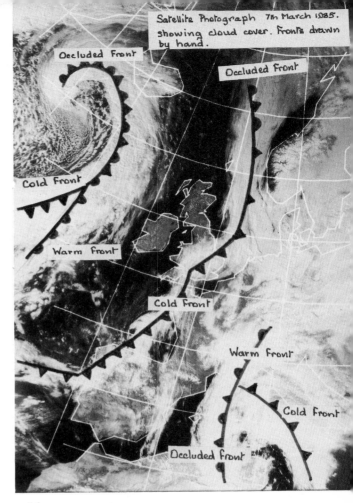

Satellite Photograph 7th March 1985, showing cloud cover. Fronts drawn by hand.

Section across the low-pressure system shown on page 14.

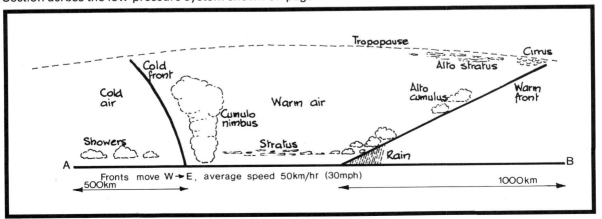

Fronts move W→E, average speed 50km/hr (30mph)

Cyclones

Cyclones are low-pressure systems with winds blowing around the low-pressure centre. They range in size from 200-km-diameter systems down to the whirlwinds or tornadoes of North America. A tropical cyclone, born in the tropics, is powered by hot, moist rising air. As the air rises it cools until water vapour begins to condense to form droplets of water. The change from gaseous water vapour to liquid water is accompanied by the release of heat energy. This release of energy is vast and powers the air to rise even faster. At the centre of the storm – the calm "eye" – air is sinking and, as it falls earthwards, it heats up because of the increase in pressure. Meanwhile, in the swirling outer parts, the winds reach speeds of well above 100 mph (150 km hr^{-1}).

Tropical cyclones travel mostly over warm tropical seas which supply the energy needed. Cut off from a ready source of tropical energy the hurricane becomes the familiar low-pressure system arriving over Britain some week or fortnight after it has ravaged the Caribbean.

Another spinning column of air, only this time on a very much smaller scale, is the Twister or tornado of the USA. These are tubes of rapidly revolving air which spread destruction whenever and wherever they touch the ground. The tube, similar to the one in the

Circles show temperatures expected in Fahrenheit. The equivalent temperature in Centigrade is given in brackets. Arrows indicate wind direction and speed in mph. Pressures in millibars and inches. Note that the winds in a cyclone/low pressure system move in an anti-clockwise direction around the low pressure centre.

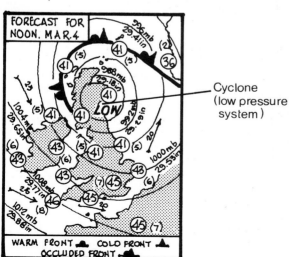

Cyclone (low pressure system)

photograph, may be only a few hundred metres in diameter but the air revolving round it quite likely reaches speeds of above 200 mph (320 km hr^{-1}). Not only are there high winds but the pressure inside the tube is abnormally low and so the passage of a tornado over houses causes the houses to blow apart. Then, of course, the vicious wind tears the structures to pieces. The photograph above shows how trees on a farm in North Carolina were flattened when a tornado hit the area in 1984. The pickup truck had been blown in to the wooded area by the storm. The danger from tornadoes is so great in some of the Mid-West states of the USA that strongly reinforced "cyclone cellars" are built beneath houses as storm shelters.

Hurricanes and tornadoes need energy to power them. This comes from the Sun and so we would expect them to be more common in the summer and early autumn. This is the hurricane season, and the USA Weather Bureau keeps a close watch for the development of storms. Nowadays satellite pictures monitor the development of weather systems and warnings can be sent to areas at risk.

The Whys and Wherefores of hurricanes are still largely unknown, although more and more information is being collected. Pilots in special aeroplanes fly into the whirling winds, measuring temperatures and wind speeds at different heights, and this enables scientists to construct models of the whirling giants.

Anticyclones

Anticyclones are just the opposite of cyclones. Cyclones are restless, turbulent whirlpools of energy, while anticyclones are quiet, peaceful areas of high pressure. In summer they produce fine weather – light winds and clear, sunny skies, attracting thousands of people to the beaches. The winter anticyclone is associated with frosts and, if the air is moist, the formation of fogs.

The scientific reasons for the weather associated with anticyclones are these. An anticyclone is an area of sinking air. Air from the top of the troposphere, and which is cold and dry, slowly sinks and, as it does so, becomes denser because of the increase in air pressure (the air pressure decreases as you ascend, increases as you descend). This increase in pressure causes the air to warm up. Warm air can contain more water vapour than cold air, and so the cold, dry air that has warmed up becomes capable of holding more water vapour. In fact, the air does not contain enough water vapour for it to condense at the temperature of the air at which you might expect clouds to form, and the result is that clouds are rarer.

In winter an anticyclone is a mixed blessing. Clear skies enable the ground to radiate heat back into space and so the ground cools rapidly; clouds, on the other hand, act as blankets and keep the ground warm. So, during an anti-cyclone, the ground becomes colder than the air above it. When the air is cooled below the temperature at which the water vapour condenses, droplets of water are formed and so a fog or mist is produced. Such a mist or fog is called a radiation fog.

Calm and cloudless nights are conditions favourable for frost, but not all frosts are associated with anticyclones. Frosts can be the result of cold polar air brought to us by a

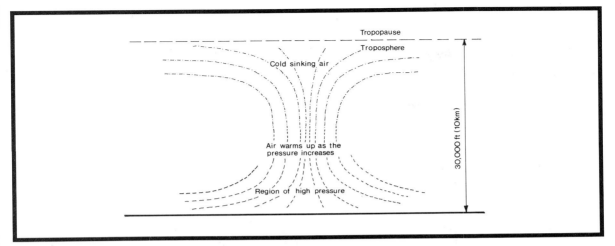

Vertical section through an anticyclone.

depression. These conditions are usually short-lived.

Air moves around an anticyclone in a clockwise direction. Sometimes an anticyclone seems to get stuck or, as it slowly drifts away, its place is taken by another. If an anticyclone

Note that the winds in an anticyclone move in a clockwise direction around the high pressure system. The wind velocities are very much lower than the cyclone wind velocity. (See the diagram on page 16).

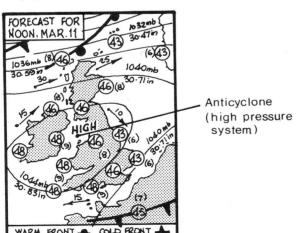

Anticyclone (high pressure system)

becomes stuck to the north or northeast of Britain, it directs winds over the country from the north or the Continent. In the summer the result is long periods of dry, sunny weather. In the winter the east winds from the cold Continent make us shiver. These "stuck" anti-cyclones are called "blocking anticyclones" because they stop the passage eastwards of the low-pressure cyclones, which would bring rain and cloudy conditions.

Quite often we find a blocking anticyclone centred over the Azores. It is slow-moving and can remain there for weeks. While it is there it directs cyclones round its northern edge, giving us our typical, changeable weather.

Every evening on TV the weather man presents charts showing the barometric pressure all over the British Isles. Lines are drawn on the charts connecting points of equal pressure – they look rather like the contour lines on maps, which connect points of equal height. Barometric pressure is measured by a barometer (see page 36). A continuous record can be made of barometric pressure using a barograph. This produces a chart showing the air pressure at a particular place throughout a week. An example of a barograph chart and its association with the weather map is shown on page 39.

Mists, Fogs and Smogs

There is a simple explanation for all mists and fogs. They occur when air containing water vapour is cooled and reaches a temperature at which the vapour condenses, either as small droplets of water or as ice crystals. This temperature is called the dewpoint. Clouds are only mists or fogs high up in the air. On page 18 mention was made of radiation fog, formed when the ground radiates heat into clear skies. Another type of fog is found where the ground or sea is colder than the dewpoint of the air above

it and the moist air is moving in from a warmer area. This is called an advection fog. The movement of air can be due to cooled air rolling down a hillside into even colder areas or, as is most likely, to a gentle breeze bringing warmer, moist air into a cold region.

Every year we see on TV News the results of multiple road crashes on motorways. Usually the accidents have happened because of alternate banks of fog and good visibility. The photograph shows some of the wreckage after a pile-up which happened in fog on the M6 in September 1971. More than 200 vehicles were involved, ten people were killed and 60 injured.

Smog is a mixture of the worst elements of smoke and fog. It is fog droplets and particles of substances other than water. London was a city plagued by smogs for hundreds of years. The burning of sea-coal was blamed for the "presumptuous smoke" by the diarist John Evelyn who lived during the reign of Charles II (1660-85). Evelyn went on to say that Londoners "breathe nothing but an impure and thick mist, accompanied by a fuliginous and filthy vapour, corrupting the lungs, so that catarrhs, coughs and consumptions rage more in this one city, than in the whole Earth". The London pea-souper, as it was called, was described by Charles Dickens in the opening paragraphs of *Bleak House*. It has been the setting for countless film dramas of Victorian England. In spite of complaints, the winter smogs were accepted until 1952.

On Friday, 5 December of that year Londoners woke to a dawn that never came. A thick pea-souper blanketed London. Cold, damp and murky, it encouraged people to stoke up their coal fires. Soon the air was thick with coal-fire smoke – small particles of ash, droplets of tar and the choking gas sulphur dioxide. The

sulphur dioxide combined with the water droplets and oxygen in the air to form drops of sulphuric acid. Probably 4,000 people died from the effects of the smog. A medical journal reported that the number of deaths in the four days of the smog exceeded the number who had died in the same period of time during the cholera epidemic of 1866.

The condition which produced four days without a dawn is known as a temperature inversion. Covering London was a shallow layer of cold air. Over the top of this, just like a lid on a saucepan, was air that was warmer than the surface layer. Into the cold surface layer were poured all the waste gaseous products of homes and industries. They couldn't get away. Warm air on top of cold is the reverse of the normal state, where the temperature falls by about 3.5°-4.5°F for every thousand feet you go up (or, in metric units, 6°-8°C for every kilometre). Normally a bubble of warm air from a chimney, for example, will rise and continue to rise through air that is colder and denser. When there is a temperature inversion, the bubble rises until it reaches the warmer and less dense air – and there it stops.

Cities like Los Angeles (in the photograph above) and San Francisco are notorious for their smog trapped by a lid of warm air. For them the smog is not caused by coal-burning fires but by the action of sunlight on the fumes produced by thousands of cars. The chemistry of what happens is not fully understood but the results are most unpleasant.

As a result of the London smog of 1952 the British Government in 1956 introduced the Clean Air Act. The UK is gradually being converted to smokeless fuels, and the pea-soupers are no longer haunting our cities. There are still fogs, but they are fewer in number and they are not as dirty as they used to be.

The US Government has passed strict laws on the exhaust gases of cars. These set definite limits on the amount of carbon monoxide, unburnt petrol and oxides of nitrogen that a car's exhaust may contain. It seems likely that the European Parliament will also introduce regulations governing car exhaust emissions because these are thought to be one of the factors causing "Acid Rain". Cleaning the exhausts of cars will be expensive. Cars will cost more; are likely to use more petrol; and will be less efficient than the cars of today.

There is a particularly dangerous form of fog – freezing fog. Water can exist as a liquid below 0°C. It is then said to be supercoooled. Freezing fog consists of supercooled droplets. When it hits obstacles such as fences, trees and cars, some of the droplets freeze immediately, forming white, opaque ice, full of air spaces.

Snow and Blizzards

Bing Crosby made one of the most successful records of all time. His song was "I'm dreaming of a White Christmas". Our Christmas cards often have scenes of robins and snow, yet in Britain white Christmasses are rare. Our snowy weather does not really start until the middle of January and it depends largely on where you live whether it will last. We have a love-hate relationship with snow. It is grand for holidays, skiing and snowball fights and looks beautiful on trees – but for animals, farmers and people getting to work, it is not so good.

Snowflakes are made up of crystals of ice. Because of the way molecules of water join together, ice crystals have shapes that are all based on either a six-pointed cross , or a hexagonal plate , or a hexagonal column sometimes capped with a pyramid . No ice crystal is based on a four-pointed cross ✕ or an eight-pointed shape ✳. The shape of the ice crystals depends on the temperature at which the crystals form.

The melting-point of snow or ice is lowered by any pressure. This means that ice or snow near 0°C (the melting-point at normal atmospheric pressure) will melt when squeezed, i.e. when a pressure is applied. When the pressure (squeeze) is released, the liquid freezes. This property is called regelation. It has a number of what might seem to be unconnected effects.

Snowballs can generally be made in Britain because, usually, the temperature of the snow is close to its melting point (0°C). It is difficult or impossible to make snowballs with very cold snow in North America or in Europe. Every winter we read of our railways being halted because of frozen points; roads blocked by deep drifts; airports closed because of ice on the runways. We grumble and say it never seems to happen on the Continent. It does not happen there because the winters are colder and the snow does not pack down into lumps of ice. Cold snow can be blown away and the clearing of roads, railways and airports is relatively easy.

Snowfalls often arrive in blizzard conditions with the wind piling up the snow in huge drifts. Stories have been told of the great storm of 1891 in Devon. The snow was so deep that all the

hedges were buried, and on the west side of Dartmoor one steep valley was completely filled. This would make the drift 200'-800' deep (60-250 m). Such a story has been confirmed by a number of eye-witnesses. Ask your parents and grandparents if they have any stories to tell of snow and blizzards. Ask them if they remember the winters of 1963, 1947 and 1940.

The reason for snowdrifts is that in the lee of an obstacle the speed of the wind drops and so the wind can no longer hold up the flakes of snow. Next time it snows, notice the direction of the wind and later, when it has stopped snowing, see where the drifts can be found. Along some of the main roads in northern England and Scotland snow-fences can be seen, set back a short distance from the road. These fences are just palings set about a foot apart. Wind can whistle through the gaps and spin round behind the palings, dropping its burden of snow there and not on the road.

Once snow has fallen and formed a blanket over the ground, it protects anything there from the frost. Snow is a good insulator because it is full of air. 25cm (10″) of snow when melted is equivalent to 2.5 cm (1″) of rain. Snow is a good reflector of sunlight – so much so that rarely

does sun melt snow. Thawing is most likely due to warm air brought in from warmer places by a depression.

In areas of the Earth where the amount of snow falling in the winter is greater than the amount melting in the summer, snow builds up to form snowfields. More and more accumulates until some of it begins to move downhill as a river of ice. This is the way glaciers are formed. Glaciers continue moving downhill until either they reach the sea and break off as icebergs or they reach warmer air and melt. Glaciers travel on a thin layer of water formed because the weight of the ice causes some of it to melt. Exactly the same principle is responsible for the ease with which skaters glide over the ice. The blade of the skate causes a thin layer of water to form between the skate and the ice.

As you climb a mountain it steadily becomes colder, at a rate of 6°-8°C per kilometre, until you reach a region where there is a permanent cover of snow. The junction between snow and no-snow is called the snowline. In the British Isles the tops of the highest mountains in Scotland are just below the snowline although snow has been seen on the Cairngorm Mountains in Scotland in July and August.

Rain and Hail

The rain it raineth on the just
and also on the unjust fella:
But chiefly on the just, because
The unjust steals the just's umbrella
(Lord Bowers, 1835-1894)

Rain, the stuff we take for granted until a drought comes along, is a source of puzzlement to scientists. Rain falls from clouds, but how do drops of rain form? To make the question clearer let's look at the whole process of rain-making. The starting-point is water on the surface of the Earth, either in the oceans, lakes and ponds or in the soil. Energy from the Sun changes liquid water into water vapour. This change requires energy, a fixed amount for every gram of water evaporated. This amount is called the Latent Heat of Vaporization and is equal to 2.26 Kjoules g^{-1}.

Water-vapour-laden air is lighter than dry air and as it rises it expands. Air that expands becomes colder. If the rate of cooling is so quick that the rising air is not warmed by the surrounding air, then the temperature falls by about 10°C for every kilometre ascended. This rate of cooling continues until the dewpoint is reached. The dewpoint is the temperature at which moisture starts to condense from the water vapour. It varies according to the amount of water vapour in the air: the drier the air the lower the dewpoint. The droplets of water formed are very small, about one hundredth of a millimetre in diameter, and although they fall, it is only very, very slowly. The puzzle is, how do small droplets grow into raindrops?

There are two theories. In 1933 Tor Harold Percival Bergeron, a Swedish meteorologist, suggested that raindrops were melted snow and ice particles. Often the temperature inside clouds falls well below 0°C. Droplets of water do not freeze unless there are small solid particles to act as nuclei. If there are some particles like this then ice crystals form around them. The supercooled droplets that have not turned into ice evaporate and the water vapour formed is condensed on the ice crystals, causing them to grow. The ice crystals collide and coalesce to form snowflakes. When these are large enough they fall and if they reach areas where the temperature is above 0°C (32°F), they melt and fall as rain; otherwise they fall as snow.

This was a nice theory but it did not explain why sometimes rain fell from clouds in which the temperature was above 0°C (32°F) at all times. Irving Langmuir, an American chemist, suggested that when there are droplets of different sizes within a cloud, the larger ones collide with the smaller ones as they fall. So the larger droplets grow bigger and the smaller ones are eliminated. This theory requires that there should be droplets of different sizes. Droplets form around solid nuclei and if these are of different sizes, so too will be the droplets. Nuclei may be dust particles or small crystals of common salt formed by the evaporation of sea-spray. This theory explains rain falling from warm clouds in the tropics.

And now for hail. Hailstones come in many sizes. Some are small like peas, some are as big as cricket-balls and when these fall they cause havoc. In India in 1888, hundreds of people were killed by hailstones. In 1360, an English army outside Paris lost so many men and horses, killed by hailstones, that King Edward III agreed to sign the Peace of Bretigny, which brought to an end part I of the Hundred Years War between England and France. The destructive power of a hail-storm is truly frightful; it can reduce standing crops and fruit trees to trash – in less time than it takes to tell you.

Hailstones are formed inside clouds that have violent, up-and-down winds within them. Ice pellets are tossed up and down; in the lower regions of the cloud water condenses on the ice drop and then freezes as the hailstone is tossed high into the upper part of the cloud. The process continues until the hailstones grow to such a size and weight that they cannot be supported by upwards-blowing winds. Down they come, the big ones reaching speeds of well over 150 km/hr (100 mph), smashing crops, animals, people, roofs and even cars.

The clouds in which hailstones are formed are the towering Cumulonimbus – the thunder-clouds that climb 10 km (30,000 feet) and conceal within a shiny white overcoat a vicious black heart.

If a sphere is allowed to fall through air or a liquid, it speeds up and finally reaches its terminal velocity – the highest speed it reaches. Terminal velocity depends largely on the mass and size of the falling object. A heavy, small object will fall faster than a light, large object; a golf ball will fall faster than a balloon. Only in the absence of air, such as on the Moon, will a feather fall as fast as a cannonball.

25

Frosts and Freezing

During the winter, land away from the sea becomes very much colder than land bordering on the sea. This is because water holds on to heat much more readily than the land; also, currents in the Atlantic Ocean bring to us in Britain warm water from the southwest. The west wind drift keeps us much milder than similar latitudes of northeast America. Winter brings cold conditions to central Europe and, if the wind is in the east, cold winds chill us.

East winds from Russia are often brought to Britain by an anticyclone centred over Scandinavia. If the anticyclone becomes stuck – a blocking anticyclone – then we are in for a cold period. Winds are dry and cold and if the anti-cyclone to the northeast of us develops at the same time as low-pressure systems are to the south of us, then the wind can become strong. Depressions approaching Britain from the southwest are either blocked or fended off to the south. Sometimes a low moves into northern France or central Europe causing widespread snow with some of the effects being brought to us by the east wind.

During the last one hundred years the coldest winters have been in 1895, 1897, 1940, 1947 and 1963, with 1963 being probably the coldest since 1684 which was the coldest recorded winter. During the "great frost" of 1963 which lasted from Christmas Day 1962 until March 1963, the cold in Bath, Avon, for example, was so intense that water-mains under the roads froze and on one building site the ground was found to be frozen to a depth of 27″ (70 cm). Permanently frozen ground, known as permafrost, occurs in Canada and Siberia. The greatest depth of permafrost is 4,920′ (1500 m) in the river Lena basin, Siberia.

During prolonged cold weather lakes and then rivers freeze and curling, one of Scotland's national games, can be enjoyed. In England, when the Fens freeze, ice-skating races are held. Three times in the past 300 years the River Thames has frozen so hard that fairs have been held on the ice. The second illustration shows the Great Frost Fair of 1683.

Water is a curious stuff. When it cools it contracts until the temperature falls to 4°C. Then, as the temperature falls still further, water starts to expand. At 0°C it freezes and expands still further. Let us see what effects this strange property has. A pond of water cools and cold water sinks, leaving warmer water at the surface until all the water is at 4°C. Then only the top layer cools any further because water at a temperature between 4° and 0°C is lighter than water at 4°C. So the top layer cools and freezes, leaving the rest of the water at 4°C. The pond only cools further by the ice on top conducting heat to the surface. Ponds and lakes freeze from the surface and unless the cold is

prolonged and severe there is water for fishes to live in under the ice.

What is the explanation of this phenomenon? Molecules of water have a shape like this:

The forces joining the atoms together are electrical in nature but they leave the oxygen part of the molecule slightly negative and the hydrogen parts slightly positive. Overall, the molecule is neutral. The slightly negative part of one molecule attracts the slightly positive part of another molecule. A weak link is formed, called a "hydrogen bond". As water is cooled below 4°C more and more water molecules are linked together. The joined molecules occupy more space than the unjoined molecules all taken together. So the water appears to expand because the expansion due to the molecules joining together is greater than the contraction due to cooling. Finally, when water freezes, the solid structure formed occupies more space than did all the separate bits before freezing. It is like a stack of bricks about to be built into a house.

The house occupies more space than all the separate bricks.

It is the expansion when water freezes that causes havoc with the water-pipes. Frost causes hard rocks to split because water in cracks freezes, expands and drives the crack deeper. So, at the bottom of cliffs, we find screes of sharp, angular rocks, which have broken off the cliff face.

Besides the cold weather brought to us from polar regions or the cold-hearted Continent, we can get frost under other conditions. On nights when there is no cloud and no wind, the ground radiates its warmth back into space. A radiation frost follows. Cold air can roll down a hillside, filling a valley and creating a frost hollow. There is a notorious frost hollow at Rickmansworth, Hertfordshire. Here a natural valley is blocked by a railway embankment. Cold air, being denser than warm air, rolls down the hillside, filling the valley with freezing air. Frost hollows are of particular concern to fruit-growers and market-gardeners in the spring. A number of methods have been tried to protect fruit blossom from frost. These range from building walls to deflect the cold air, to lighting fires and even spraying the blossom with water.

Often in deserts, where the daytime temperature can be well above 100°F (38°C), the night-time temperature may drop to freezing.

Floods and Droughts

Most of the time, floods and droughts are cases of too much or too little of a good thing. However, for India, the season of the monsoon rains means that rice can be planted in the flooded paddy-fields and life can go on. Without the southwest monsoon, bringing moisture-laden air across the Indian Ocean, India would lie baked brown and crops would shrivel and die. Egypt has relied for life upon the Nile for six thousand years. Yearly the river flooded, spreading water and silt across the fields on either side. The very existence of the peasant depended on the yearly flood – no flood, no food, no life.

Both India and Egypt have depended on the right weather at the right time. In India the rains themselves bring the floods. Egypt sees little rain. It depends upon the rains and snows falling on the land near to the sources of the Nile

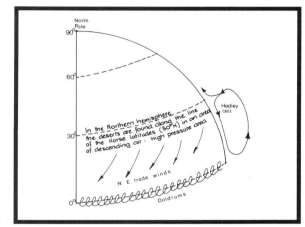

Deserts in the Northern Hemisphere.

and for thousands of years the reason for the river's annual flooding was hidden because no one had traced it back to Ethiopia and Lake Victoria.

At present, the world is beset by the spectre of drought and famine. Right across Africa, just south of the Sahara, the rains have failed, crops have died and people and cattle have starved. No one is quite sure what has happened, why there should be such a long period of drought. The result has been catastrophic. Thousands have died. Thousands upon thousands of square miles of country have become desert, unable to support the meanest of vegetation and unlikely to be of any use if and when the rains return.

It seems that the high-pressure belt along the Horse latitudes has moved south. This high pressure is caused by the sinking air of the Hedley cell. As the air sinks from high altitude it heats up and becomes drier and so is less likely to form rain clouds. Those clouds that do form come from moisture dried out of the

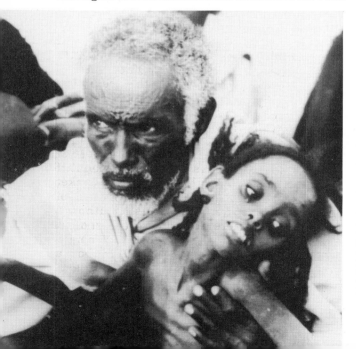

parched ground. The earth gets drier and still no rains come. Under these conditions crops fail, ground vegetation, bushes and ultimately even the trees die. The earth is laid bare to the scouring action of the wind. Soil is blown away, leaving rocks, stones and sterile sand. The land is useless even if the rains do return. North African deserts are steadily advancing southwards, swallowing up what has been fertile and productive ground. So it is, that a temporary change of climate can have a permanent effect on the landscape and the people who used to live there.

Floods, too, can have a fearful effect. In China one million people were drowned when floods changed the course of the Yellow River in 1852. It used to flow to the south of Shantung. Now it reaches the sea 300 miles northwest of its old mouth. Every year, in some place, flood disasters occur to a greater or lesser extent. Too much rain in the hills will swell rivers until the lands by them are covered by dirty brown water.

Weather conditions can cause floods of a different kind. In 1953 the sea defences of East Anglia, Essex and Holland were breached and sea-water poured in, flooding many miles of low-lying land and drowning over 2,000 people. The reason for this flood was a combination of circumstances. There was a very high tide and this coincided with a deep depression moving across the North Sea. With a depression the height of the sea rises because there is less pressure pushing down on the sea. There were also high winds from the north. All these factors combined to produce a tidal surge, a super-high tide that topped sea-walls and then tore great gaps in them. Not only were many people drowned; 80,000 people were made homeless and it took a long time to repair the sea defences and rid the soil of sea-salt. The photograph shows the magnitude of the task which faced the people of Jaywick in Essex, England. The force of the flood which tore through the sea defences ripped the wooden chalets from their foundations and jumbled them together.

London has been threatened by high tides a number of times in the past fifty years and on several occasions has escaped disaster by only

an inch or so. A little higher tide, and floodwater would have poured down into the Underground railway tunnels. So grave was the situation likely to be that it was decided to build a "pop-up" barrage at Greenwich to close the river Thames against a tidal surge. Normally the barrage lies flat on the bed of the river. But, when danger threatens, the huge steel barrage doors are brought up into position, preventing the tide from surging up the river and overwhelming the walls along the riverside. On 25 May 1983, the British Post Office issued a 20½p stamp commemorating the opening of the Thames Barrage scheme.

So it is a combination of high tide, northerly wind and a low-pressure system that could put the sea defences along the east coast of Britain into danger. There are two other factors not yet mentioned. 15,000 years ago a large amount of Britain and Europe was buried under a blanket of ice. Then the ice began to melt and the level of the sea began to rise. It is still rising although now very much more slowly. Also, the whole of Britain is tilting. The southeast corner is sinking at the rate of about 30 cm (1 foot) a century and the northwest corner is rising at the same rate. All in all, a damp future is forecast for London and the southeast.

Thunder-storms and Other Electrical Phenomena

Cynically it has been said that an English summer is three sunny days and a thunder-storm! A thunder-storm is fun to watch. The vivid bolts of lightning and the crashing and rolling rumble of thunder provide a spectacle, a natural *Son et Lumière* beyond our efforts.

The huge generators of electrical power are the towering Cumulonimbus clouds that stretch upwards for 7 miles. These are the clouds that grow like the geni from the bottle into frightening giants. Within their seething cauldrons fierce winds rage up and down and huge charges of electricity build up until the electrical potential is in the order of 100 million volts. Then the pent-up energy is released in a lightning flash. This stab of energy heats a thin ribbon of air along its path to a temperature hotter than the surface of the Sun (+ 6000°C). It is the sudden expansion and then contraction on cooling of the air that produces thunder. A lightning stroke close to you gives a sharp, ear-splitting crash; one farther away is accompanied by a long, sonorous rumble as the sound is reflected off the clouds and the ground.

High-speed photographs show that a lightning flash is made up of a number of strokes following one another in rapid succession. First of all a "leader stroke" prepares the way and this is followed by the main flash, the "return stroke". After this, other strokes may take place along the same pathway as other portions of the cloud are tapped.

Inside the Cumulonimbus cloud the electrical charges are separated so that the top of the cloud becomes positively charged and most of the bottom of the cloud is negatively charged. The Earth is positively charged beneath the thunder-cloud. Discharges takes place between clouds or within clouds more frequently than flashes to Earth. These internal flashes light up the clouds and are generally called sheet-lightning.

The separation of charges in a thunder-cloud is similar to the action that takes place in a Van de Graaff generator, which builds up a high voltage by carrying charges on a moving belt to a large metal globe on top of the machine. In a thunder-cloud the up-and-down flows of ice crystals carry out this function. Hail has always been associated with thunder-storms.

Why do we get thunder-storms? It is easier to ask: What weather is associated with thunder-storms? That can be fairly easily answered; it is the weather that is favourable to the formation of the towering Cumulonimbus clouds.

You cannot have thunder without a lightning-producer and this is the familiar thunder-cloud. Cumulonimbus grow from cotton-wool Cumulus clouds until they reach 11 km (35,000′) and develop a flat top as they meet the Tropopause. This growth requires that there should be a plentiful supply of warm, moist air at ground level and something to set off the growth. This trigger may be extra-strong thermals or turbulence due to air flow from the sea. The approach of a cold front, with the cold air undercutting the warm, can set off lines of thunder-clouds (known in the USA as Line Squalls).

St Elmo's Fire is an electrical phenomenon which used to scare sailors. It is a flickering bluish light that appears at the ends of masts and spars of ships and of aeroplane propellers. This electrical glow is called a corona discharge

and takes place wherever there is a build-up of electrical charge at a pointed surface. Although it is harmless, it does show that high electrical potentials are present and that a thunder-storm is likely.

A rare form of lightning which has never been explained is ball lightning. An eye-witness reported: "We were sitting down to tea with the french windows open. It was a hot sultry day with occasional rumbles of thunder. Suddenly a yellow-orange ball, a little smaller than a football, floated in through the open window. Crossing the room, it passed between us, then dipped and disappeared up the chimney. Although it could only have taken a couple of seconds, it seemed half a lifetime." No one has explained what ball lightning is; sometimes it explodes with a large bang; sometimes it just fades away; generally it seems to avoid touching people.

Structure of a thunder-cloud (Cumulonimbus).

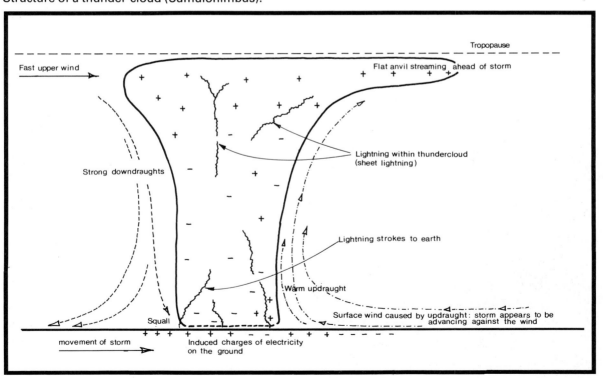

Rainbows and Haloes

I do set my bow . . . . upon the earth.
(Genesis 9, v.13-16)

A rainbow with its array of colours is delightful and well-known. The colours range from red to violet – but if you draw a bow, which colour is on the inside and which is on the outside? You can see for yourself the next time there is a rainbow. How is a rainbow formed? The answer to this question depends on observations made by Sir Isaac Newton three hundred years ago. He passed a shaft of sunlight through a prism and shone the emergent light onto a white wall. The wall displayed a range of colours from red to violet. The angle by which light is bent when passed through a prism is called the angle of deviation and this is less for red light than for violet. The whole process of light bending when it passes from one transparent substance to another (for example, from air to glass or from

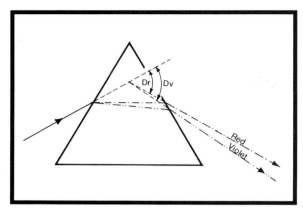

Deviation of light through a prism. Dv is the deviation of violet light. Dr is the deviation of red light. Dv > Dr.

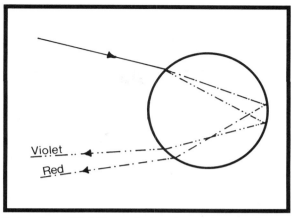

Refraction of light in a raindrop to produce a primary bow.

air to water) is known as refraction. A rainbow is formed both by refraction of sunlight through raindrops and by reflection of sunlight off raindrops. It can only be seen by a person standing with his or her back to the Sun.

Sometimes when you see a rainbow you may see another one outside it. The inside rainbow is called the primary bow. It usually has the more intense colours and red is the outside colour. The larger bow is called the secondary bow and red is the inside colour. This bow has muted colours. To explain the formation of the two bows let us assume that a raindrop is spherical.

Refraction of light in a raindrop to produce a secondary bow.

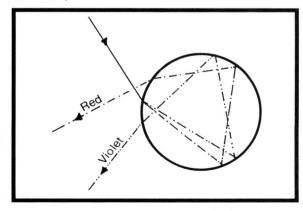

In a primary rainbow sunlight follows a path through falling raindrops, as shown above. The result is that the light has been refracted twice, once on entering and then on leaving the raindrop. It has also been reflected once inside the drop. Red light has been refracted and reflected to a lesser amount than violet light and appears on the outside of the bow.

With a secondary bow, light entering the raindrop is refracted and is then reflected *twice* inside the drop. Finally it is refracted again on leaving the raindrop. A secondary bow is therefore less bright than the accompanying primary bow.

The higher the Sun is in the sky, the lower is the arch of the rainbow until, when the Sun is higher than approximately 53°, the bow cannot be seen at ground level.

Just as drops of water refract (bend) light, so will ice crystals. The commonest effects are haloes round the Sun or the Moon, produced when they are veiled by a thin sheet of the ice-crystal cloud, Cirrostratus.

The appearance of haloes is taken by country-folk to indicate rain. There is some truth in the belief because Cirrostratus, which produces haloes, precedes a frontal system containing rain. However, the front may die out, or the halo may be caused by a patch of Cirrus cloud not connected with a front.

Ancient Weather

Surprisingly, we know quite a lot about the weather of the past – not just the weather of last year or of last century but that of millions of years ago. When we talk about past weather we need two things. We need to know *when* it happened and *what* happened. In other words, we need some means of dating an event, and we need to discover some way by which that event is recorded for us.

We are able to date an historical event because we have clocks and calendars and agree to start from a fixed point in time. We can employ a number of clocks, depending on how far into the past we want to go. The table shows some methods of dating the past.

Counting and matching annual growth rings in trees: Dendrochronology.

Counting varves (annual layers of sediments deposited in some glacial lakes as a result of the spring melting of ice).

Studying cores of ice/snow taken from icefields in Greenland and Antarctica.
Cores of deep-sea muds.
(Precise dating of some layers possible because of known volcanic activity and first atomic bombs.)

Measuring radioactive elements in substances. Radioactive elements decay into elements of lighter atomic mass. If we know the rate of radioactive decay of potassium into argon, for example, then assuming that a deposit contained no argon to start with, its age can be determined by measuring the argon present.

An overall picture of the weather at a time in the past can be obtained by looking at the animal and vegetable life existing at that time. We know much about prehistoric animals and plants because of fossils, not only the obvious kinds of fossils but also microscopic ones. Many plants produce pollen, and pollen grains from prehistoric times can be found preserved in peat and mud. If we can identify these pollen grains, we can tell what kinds of trees and plants were growing then. We know the kind of conditions under which trees and plants will grow. The vegetation of an area depends on its weather. So we can make deductions about the weather in the past.

The rocks themselves provide us with evidence. Sandstones such as those found near Penrith and Carlisle are made up of smooth, rounded grains of sand, all about the same size. These sandstones were formed from what was once desert sand. Limestones made of coral remains, such as those of Wenlock Edge in Shropshire, indicate there was a warm sea. The scratched and rounded rocks of the Lake District tell the story of ice and glaciers when large areas of Northern Europe were blanketed in ice and cold, while dry tundra conditions existed over much of the rest.

Over the past three million years the Earth has undergone periods of arctic conditions over much of Europe and North America; semi-tropical conditions over the same areas; and enormous variations in the level of the oceans. At one time the North Sea was dry land covered with conifer forests and the Straits of Dover did not exist. *Homo sapiens* could have walked on dry land all the way from what is now Penzance, England through Europe, Asia and North America to New York. Look it up in an atlas and see how it could be done.

The ice ages alternated with warm periods and during the period 3.25 million years BP (before the present) to 120,000 years BP there were about 34 periods of glaciation with warm intermissions. Since then there has been one prolonged period of ice-age conditions with

glaciers and ice-sheets covering much of the land in Europe above latitude 55°N and in North America about 40°-48°N. The ice-sheets of the last ice age reached a maximum extent about 18,000 years BP, burying the land in a white blanket thousands of metres thick. Only the tops of mountains stuck through the ice. These ice-sheets robbed the oceans of their water, because they grew and grew and ice piled up on top of more ice, so lowering the sea level by as much as 300 m. South of the ice-sheets were cold semi-deserts inhabited by beasts adapted to face these conditions. By this time our own species of man had evolved and *homo sapiens sapiens* hunted the mammoth, arctic fox, woolly rhinoceros, musk ox, bison and elk. About 10,000 BP the weather suddenly changed for the better and the ice-sheets melted. Humankind changed from being merely hunters to being animal herders and later crop cultivators. The Lapps of Finland and Sweden still follow the animal migration of the reindeer just as their ancestors must have done thousands of years ago. In North America the Red Indians belonged to a hunting society until about a hundred years ago. The Eskimos still live by hunting seals.

A valuable way of determining the temperature of long ago is to analyse snow and ice laid down at the time and preserved in the permanent snowfields of Greenland and Antarctica. The oxygen in the air is made up of oxygen which has an atomic mass of 16 and a very small amount of oxygen with an atomic mass of 18. Both forms of oxygen have the same chemical properties, but they have slightly different physical properties. Compounds of the two forms of oxygen also differ only in their physical properties. Water containing oxygen, atomic mass 18, does not evaporate so easily as the common form of water (with oxygen 16).

The ice-sheets increased during the ice ages, and water was removed from the oceans. Water with oxygen 16 is more volatile than water containing oxygen 18, and so during cold weather the ice- and snowfields were formed with snow having a larger percentage of oxygen 16. The percentage of heavy oxygen gives an indication of the temperature; the smaller the proportion of oxygen 18 the colder the temperature was.

The reasons for ice-age conditions probably lie in variations in the Earth's orbit round the Sun and variations in the Earth's tilt relative to the Sun. This hypothesis was suggested by the Yugoslavian scientist Milutin Milankovitch sixty years ago. Knowing the variations in orbit and tilt, the average weather can be calculated for a position on the Earth at any time in the past million years. The theoretic values agree very well with those obtained from [18]0 determinations.

Measuring the "Elements"

Figures make the world go round. We count the pence in our pockets, the number of grams of flour in a cake, the gallons or litres of petrol we buy at a garage; everything seems to be tied to figures. The same applies to weather. Was the hottest day last year hotter than the hottest day a century ago? Without figures and measurements we cannot say. We need to measure the elements of weather.

Nowadays we measure the speed of the wind, air pressure, air temperature and its humidity (dryness or wetness) in units that are accepted worldwide and by methods that are reliable.

Air pressure was the first measurement to be made and this was done using a mercury barometer.

In many homes there is a barometer hanging on the wall. Most likely, this instrument is an aneroid barometer. It does not contain mercury but has inside a thin corrugated-metal box from which the air has been pumped. A variation in the atmospheric pressure causes the end of the box to move in or out. This movement is magnified by levers which move a pointer over a scale. If there is a barometer like this in your home, in what units does it measure barometric pressure?

A lever used as a movement magnifier.

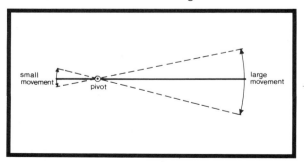

A barograph like the one above is used to make a continuous record of every variation in barometric pressure over a period of time. It is based on the aneroid principle but moves a pen over a very-slowly-moving strip of paper instead of a pointer round a dial.

One thing that must not be forgotten when comparing atmospheric pressures at different places is the influence of altitude. All barometric measurements must be corrected to what they would be at sea-level.

The temperature of something can be measured using a thermometer and is expressed in some convenient units. S.I. units (Système International d'Unitée) use degrees Kelvin which are the same size as degrees Celsius but have a different starting-point: thus the freezing-point of water is 273.15 K or 0°C. A practical scale which is a long time dying is the Fahrenheit scale of temperature. Named after G.D. Fahrenheit (1686-1736), it is still used in everyday life in Britain, North America and most of what used to be the British Empire, in spite of attempts to replace it by the Celsius scale.

How do you measure the temperature on a hot day? If you hang a thermometer in the sun the radiant heat warms up the thermometer to a temperature higher than that of the air. If you want to measure the air temperature, then the thermometer must be hung in the shade.

Rainfall is measured by collecting rain in a jar. The units in which it is measured, inches or mm, are units of length and refer to the depth of water that would be formed if the rain falling on a flat surface did not run away. Unfortunately, the siting of the collecting vessel influences the amount of rain-water collected. It is quite

instructive to put out a number of tin cans and collect the rain from different sites. Try by walls or hedges, in the lee of buildings and out in the open in the middle of a football pitch. The depth of water in the cans can be measured by dipping a ruler into the water.

Wind velocity is also measured. There are a number of methods for doing this. The simplest was devised by an English Admiral, Sir F. Beaufort (1774-1857), in the early nineteenth century. He gave a number of descriptions of the effects of winds of different speeds on the sails of ships and the sea waves. His scale has been adapted for use on land. Nowadays meteorologists use anemometers (one is shown on the left) which often consist of cups attached to a shaft which drives an electrical generator. This produces an electric voltage that can be measured by a voltmeter. Recording voltmeters are used to keep a record over a period of time.

Other measurements of the "elements" are made. At any particular temperature air can contain only a certain amount of water vapour; then the air is saturated. Usually air contains only a percentage of the amount of water vapour that it could contain. This percentage is called the relative humidity. The simplest instrument for measuring relative humidity is the wet and dry bulb thermometer. This consists of two thermometers, one of which has its mercury bulb wrapped in a piece of damp muslin. The other thermometer is not modified in any way. As water evaporates from the muslin, energy is required to convert the water into vapour. This energy, called the latent heat of evaporation, is supplied by the water, the muslin and the thermometer. The result is that the temperature falls. By consulting tables which link air temperature, the difference between the dry and wet bulb thermometers and humidity, the relative humidity can be found.

Weather Maps and Weather Prediction

Before a weather forecaster can begin work he or she must have facts. These come from weather stations all over the Northern Hemisphere. Ships and aeroplanes also send in observations. Weather stations make observations not only at ground level, but also about eight of them in Great Britain use balloons to measure wind velocities and pressure, temperature and humidity at different heights. The balloons are fitted with radar reflectors so that they can be tracked during their flight and the wind velocity determined. They also carry a radio-sonde, a piece of apparatus used to transmit radio signals giving details of the pressure, temperature and humidity. In the photograph a radio-sonde balloon is being released. Earth satellites relay pictures showing cloud cover to specially equipped meteorological stations.

In Britain the Central Meteorological Office in Bracknell, Berkshire, is connected with meteorological offices all over the Northern Hemisphere. Nowadays so much information flows into Bracknell that it is impossible to deal with it by hand. The data is fed into a powerful computer which prepares charts showing existing atmospheric pressures like contours on a map, and also makes predictions about future depositions of pressure. The computer is programmed to employ equations of motion, aerodynamics and thermodynamics and, taking account of what has happened in the immediate past, predicts weather patterns for the future. The accuracy of any computer depends on the accuracy of the input data and on the number of observations logged. Some incorrect forecasts are inevitable because of insufficient or inaccurate data.

The computer provides charts showing the movements of fronts, cyclones and anti-cyclones: the forecaster then interprets them and makes forecasts covering limited areas of the country. For example, the computer may track the progress of an active warm front as it approaches southwest Ireland and then predict that it will cross South Wales and southern England 24 hours later. The forecaster is given the speed of advance (say 45 km/hr or 30 mph) and the width of the front (about 800 km or 500 miles). So, knowing the pattern of weather associated with the front, he or she can predict the gradual deterioration of the weather and the time of the arrival of rain in various places.

A weather map of the British Isles can be

drawn, showing at a particular time, for example, isobars (lines joining places with equal barometric pressure), wind velocities, temperatures and a number of other items of information. Such a map is called a synoptic chart and is a bird's-eye view of the weather over a whole region. Like an Ordnance Survey map, it has a number of symbols on it and these have been internationally agreed.

Looking at nightly TV weather charts, we are apt to forget that weather occupies three dimensions and that the wind and weather at ground level may be completely different from at 3 km or 10,000 feet. This can often be confirmed by looking at the clouds. There may be low-level clouds bustling along in one direction while, thousands of feet above, strings of clouds float along lazily in quite another direction. It is this 3D effect that makes weather prediction such an uncertain business. Computers help, but British forecasters need bigger and better computers and more and more observations, before they can present an accurate forecast for even the day ahead. As for long-range forecasts, they are often no more than intelligent guesses.

Barograph readings made at Bathampton, Avon, March 1985. The chart is calibrated in inches of mercury. The barograph records how a high pressure area declines and moves away before an advancing depression. The weather maps show the fronts, barometric pressure and winds for 19-22 March 1985.

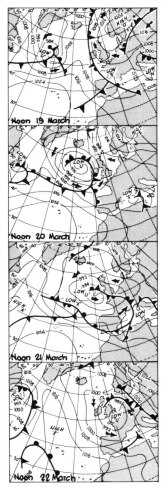

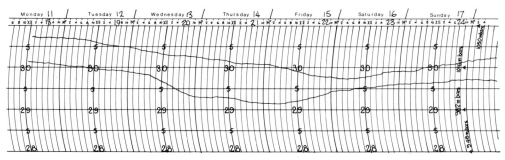

Worldly Weather

If we look at the weather in the British Isles, although it seems to change from day to day, a distinct pattern can be seen. We live in a current of mainly westerly, moist winds; our summers are not too hot and our winters are not too cold. Our climate is equable and is influenced by the sea surrounding us. This sea acts as a "thermal flywheel". In the winter it contributes heat which it has stored up during the summer. In summertime the sea is cooler than the land and so winds blowing over it are cooled. Another important factor governing Britain's climate is its position north of the Equator. The Sun is never directly overhead. Even on the longest day, the Sun is only just over 60° high in the sky. On the shortest day, the Sun does not climb even

to 15°. Then the Sun's rays have a long passage through the atmosphere. Therefore, when they strike the Earth in Britain, they have been robbed of much of their heat.

One other thing influences our climate: whether we live on low land or up a mountain. Roughly, for every 150 metres you climb upwards, the temperature drops 1°C. Also the wind whistles harder on mountain tops and so they can be very inhospitable places.

The climate of any place on Earth is governed by its position north or south of the Equator, its position relative to the oceans and its height above sea level. (Mount Kilimanjaro in Tanzania is just south of the Equator but the top is wreathed in glaciers and perpetual snow

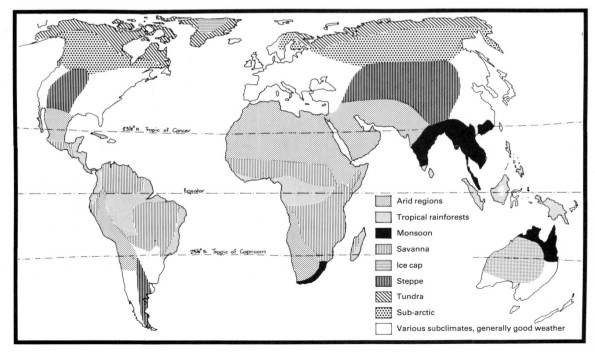

23½° N. Tropic of Cancer

Equator

23½° S. Tropic of Capricorn

- Arid regions
- Tropical rainforests
- Monsoon
- Savanna
- Ice cap
- Steppe
- Tundra
- Sub-arctic
- Various subclimates, generally good weather

because its height is 5,895 m (19, 340 ft.)

If we look at the climates of the world it might be easier to see what grows in different places; then to ask, "What is the climate?" and finally, "What are the conditions that produce such a climate?"

The first zone we will look at is one in which plants find it hard to grow. We have cold deserts and hot deserts. The cold deserts are the regions near the poles, known as tundra, or on mountains and high plateaux. They are cold because they are within the Arctic or Antarctic circles or at high altitude. Deserts are regions of low rainfall. The hot deserts are found in the southwest part of North America, much of Africa north of 10°-20°N, Arabia, Iraq, Iran, NW Pakistan. Then, in the Southern Hemisphere, there are the deserts of N Chile and Peru, SW Africa and Central Australia. The conditions for the existence of the hot deserts of the world are high pressure produced by descending air, prevailing winds that blow over large areas of land and a position near 30°N or 30°S.

The next great zone of vegetation is that of the Tropical Rainforests. These stretch across Central America, the Amazon Basin, Liberia and the Ivory Coast, the Congo Basin and the islands of the East Indies. The climate is hot and wet all the year round, just the conditions for lush vegetation. The Sun is always high in the sky at midday and so the regions receive the maximum amount of energy from the Sun. Consequently, the heated air rises, forming rain clouds and its place is taken by warm, moisture-laden air off the sea.

In America and Africa north and south of the Tropical Rainforests there are zones in which the dominant vegetation is tree-studded grasslands. Here the land experiences dry and wet seasons. The reason for this is the annual movement of the Sun. On 21 December it is overhead at the Tropic of Capricorn, 23½°S; and on 21 June it is overhead at the Tropic of Cancer, 23½°N. It drags with it the Equatorial rain-belts to produce a climate that is hot all the year round but which has wet and dry seasons. Lands with this climate and vegetation are known as Savanna regions.

Sandwiched between Savanna lands and the deserts there are belts of land with poor vegetation. This transitional zone is a semi-arid area in which rainfall varies from year to year. To the south of the Sahara Desert lie the countries of Mauritania, Mali, Niger (Burkina Faso), Chad and to the east Sudan, Ethiopia and Somalia. These are the countries of famine, where it is touch-and-go whether you live or die. If the high-pressure areas of descending dry air along the line of the 30°N latitude move south, then the rains do not arrive, the crops fail and thousands starve.

In India and South East Asia lie the lands where the vegetation grows lush and luxuriant for six months of the year and then dies back as the pitiless Sun slowly bakes the Earth. This is the land of the monsoon where the wind blows for six months from the sea, bringing water-laden clouds, and then there is a reversal of wind and for six months there is drought. The wind from the sea bringing the rains varies from year to year. Sometimes it fails and famine stalks the land; sometimes it brings too much rain and the lands are covered by a swirling sea of muddy water.

To the north of the Sahara, across Europe and the USA and in the southern parts of America, Africa and Australia are found the main grain and grassland regions. These owe their existence to the eternal battle between the cold polar airs sweeping towards the Equator and the warm, tropical, moisture-laden winds blowing polewards. There are a number of temperate climates ranging from the damp, equable weathers of the British Isles and Western Canada to the hot, dry summer climates grouped together as "Mediterranean Climates". These are found around the Mediterranean Sea, South Africa, South America, California and other parts of the USA. The controlling factors influencing the climates are: how far you are away from the sea; how near you are to the poles; and the movement north or south of the great belt of westerly winds and depressions and also the tropical high-pressure zones.

Weather and History

As we drive along our motorways over mountain and flood, or if we travel in Concorde, twice as fast as the speed of sound, we may think that humankind is master of the environment. But the forces of Nature have often decided the affairs of man. Many times has our fair and green land been covered in a thick blanket of ice and snow, driving away the inhabitants to warmer climes. As we shall see over the page, we may be living now in a warm interlude between two ice ages and, who knows, our descendants may become refugees, just like the people of the Sahel today.

Great changes in climate (as opposed to short-term changes in the weather) have favoured some people and wiped out others. During the 9th century AD the Northmen began to settle in Iceland. From about 900 AD the climate began to improve and explorers sailed westward to Greenland and to the northwest shores of mainland America. Eric the Red (Eric Röde) in the 10th century founded a colony in Greenland which grew to a population of 3,000 people, with 280 farms. From about 1130 AD the climate deteriorated and ships sailing from Iceland found it more and more difficult to make the journey. Sea ice and icebergs prevented supplies from reaching the colonists until, sometime in the 15th century, the last colonist died.

When we think of ancient civilizations we remember those of Rome, Egypt, Greece, Mesopotamia, Persia and China. There was another, less well-known one tucked away in eastern Pakistan. The cities of Harappa and Mohenjodaro dominated this region and built an advanced culture. They constructed huge granaries, grew wheat, barley, melons and dates and traded far and wide. All this started some 3000 years BC, but around about 2100 BC the civilization began to collapse as the climate became drier and colder, and former fresh-water lakes turned into salt-marshes. Productive fields became dust-bowls and a desert was born. Today this desert is advancing half a mile a year, because where plants start to grow, animals eat them and forests which grew around the desert and contained it are cut down for firewood.

These are two examples of disasters caused by long-term climatic changes. Now let's look at how history has been influenced by weather. There are many examples, in social history as well as in historical events. We all know the story of the defeat of the Spanish Armada in 1588 but did you know that King Philip of Spain made two further attempts to invade England, each of which was destroyed by storms? A typhoon smashed a Mongol invasion of Japan in 1281. A fleet of between 3000 and 4000 ships carrying 100,000 warriors was completely destroyed and all except three of the sailors and soldiers were drowned or slain.

Napoleon's defeat in 1812 was largely due to the severe cold and early snows of the winter that year. The picture shows the retreat from Moscow.

In Britain the battles of Towton (1461) and Barnet (1471), in the Wars of the Roses, were influenced by weather. In the battle of Towton, on Palm Sunday 1461, the Yorkists had the wind on their backs; the Lancastrians faced the wind and driving snow. The Yorkist army advanced and when about 300 yards short of the ranks of the Lancastrians, halted and loosed a volley of arrows. At that time the long-bow was a deadly weapon and a wound with an arrow anywhere on the body would have put an unarmoured man out of action. The Lancastrians replied but, as they shot into the wind, their arrows fell short and served as

replacement ammunition for the Yorkists. The battle raged from early morning until dark and resulted in a victory for the Yorkists, but at what a cost! Casualties on both sides were horrendous, 12,000 out of 30,000 Yorkists were killed and 20,000 out of 35,000 Lancastrians died. It was the biggest and bloodiest battle ever fought on English soil. The battle of Barnet (1471) was fought on Easter Sunday in a thick fog and could well have resulted in a victory for the Lancastrians if they could have seen their friends. As it was, they blundered and the Yorkists won.

Weather turned the Great Fire of London into a disaster. The spring and summer of 1666 were hot and dry, as a blocking anticyclone over northern Europe diverted to the south the rain-bringing depressions. By September the city was bone-dry and once the fire started it spread with devastating speed. 14,000 buildings were destroyed and 200,000 people rendered homeless.

The winter of 1709 was a terrible time and killed as many people in France as might have died in a major war. It killed livestock in their stables as well as decimating wildlife. Two-thirds of the vines and walnut trees died because of the intense cold.

The death of the walnut trees had a profound effect on the furniture trade. Walnut wood became expensive and so its place was taken by mahogany, a red-brown wood obtained from trees grown in Central America. So it was that a severe winter had its effect on the fashion of the times and you rarely find a piece of walnut furniture made after about 1720.

The new market for mahogany meant that the buccaneers, pirates and sea-rovers of many nationalities, who preyed on shipping in the Caribbean Sea, could settle down along the eastern coasts of Central America and fell and sell mahogany trees to the timber-hungry countries of Europe. Even today mahogany is felled and exported from Belize (formerly British Honduras), Honduras and Nicaragua but the buccaneers have gone. They inter-married with the native population and became "legitimate".

Whether we like it or not weather makes history. Its control of people's lives ranges from influencing where and when we take our holidays to causing the death of thousands through crop failure.

Freeze or Roast?

Here is the weather forecast for the next thousand years: "There will be spells of warm weather followed by cold, icy conditions. Further outlook uncertain and unsettled." Well, what does the future hold? Twelve thousand (12,000) years ago Britain was either buried under an ice-sheet or was a windswept, barren tundra. One hundred and twenty thousand (120,000) years ago Britain luxuriated in the warmth of an interglacial period. The onset of a series of ice ages punctuated by warm periods started about 3.25 million years ago. Since then there have been some 35 ice ages. Why do we have ice ages? What causes them? The honest answer is that we are not sure.

A Yugoslavian scientist Milutin Milankovitch in the 1920s suggested that the ice ages and their warmer intervals were caused by rhythmic changes in the Earth's orbit and the tilt of its axis. There are three cycles which interact. First, there is a regular change in the Earth's orbit round the Sun, bringing it nearer or farther away. This cycle is 90,000 years long. Second, the tilt of the Earth's axis changes between 21.8° and 24.4°. The greater the tilt, the more pronounced is the difference between summer and winter. This cycle is 40,000 years long. Thirdly, the Earth's axis wobbles. Today the Earth, during the winter in the Northern Hemisphere, is nearer the Sun than it is during the summer. In 10,000 years' time the Earth will be nearer the Sun during the Northern Hemisphere summer. This wobble is the same as can be seen with a spinning top or a gyroscope and it takes 26,000 years to complete a cycle.

These cycles reinforce or cancel out each other. Theoretical curves have been produced, predicting the temperature over a period of years and saying whether there would be an ice age or a warm interlude. The theoretical curves closely match the actual past temperatures determined from Oxygen 18 assays. What of the future? Well, it does seem that we are living in an interglacial warm period and a return of white Christmasses *and* white summers is just about due! That would be a disaster of unimaginable dimensions. Russia, Europe and North America would be buried deep under ice and snow, like Antarctica. What would happen to the inhabitants? Remember also that North America is the bread-basket of the world. It is a grim thought that famine could strike on a scale unseen ever before.

People can do nothing to influence the cycles of Nature , but we can and do have an effect on weather by dumping into the atmosphere a lot of unwanted materials. We know that volcanic dust can bring about a chilling of the climate. Mention has been made of the year without a summer (1816, see page 13), caused by the dust

blown into the atmosphere by an exploding volcano. In 1883 the eruption of Krakotoa in the Sunda Strait, near the Island of Java, also blew vast quantities of rock dust into the atmosphere. For several years afterwards European crop yields were below average because the summers were cold and damp. Dust can stop energy from the Sun from reaching us. The effect is greater in the high latitudes because rays from the Sun have to take a longer path than sunlight in the tropics, where it enters almost at right angles.

Hundreds of millions of tons of dust particles are dumped into the atmosphere by human activities every year. These come from the burning of coal; from petrol- and oil-burning cars, lorries and aeroplanes; from the ploughing of land, from the slash and burn in agriculture in Brazil, Central America and the East Indies, and from numerous other activities. All this dust helps to reflect the Sun's rays and so cool the atmosphere and bring the ice age nearer.

The "Greenhouse Effect" (see page 7) is the opposite. The glass in a greenhouse allows the Sun's energy to pour in. When it strikes the plants and things inside, the wave-length of the reflected radiation is longer than that of the incoming. Glass is not so transparent to the longer-wave radiation as to the shorter-wave-length rays. So energy is trapped and the temperature rises.

There are in the atmosphere a number of gases that can act in the same way as the glass in the greenhouse. Carbon dioxide is one such gas. It is produced as a result of burning fuels containing carbon or compounds of carbon. We know as a result of measurements made at the Mauna Loa Observatory in Hawaii, that the concentration of carbon dioxide in the atmosphere is steadily increasing (between the years 1964 and 1984, the concentration measured in December rose from 319 ppm to 331 ppm). This increase has two causes: a) the burning of carbon-based fuels, b) the cutting down and burning of the tropical rainforests.

At present, we do not know whether the warming effect of increased carbon dioxide concentration balances the cooling effects of dust and orbital variations. It is touch-and-go whether the cooling-down or the warming-up effects will win. If the world cools down, and before the onslaught of an ice age, there will be droughts in the monsoon lands and a much shorter growing season in the main food-producing areas. Already Russia is experiencing poor grain harvests, insufficient to feed her own people, and famine is stalking the Third World.

If the world warms up a few degrees, then the ice around the poles will melt. Then the extra water in the oceans will cause a rise in sea level, perhaps 60-90 metres (200-300 feet). Look at an atlas and see if your town will be under water. If it stands less than 90 m (300') above present sea level then it will be in danger of being overwhelmed by the sea. Certainly, much of the productive, crop-bearing lands will be submerged and famine will result.

I do not think that we need fear roasting. It is the cold that will chill the blood, and a fall of only 6°C in the average temperature in our latitude will usher in a new ice age.

P.S. It doesn't seem that we can win, whatever happens, not unless the scientists come up with some bright ideas. What is your solution?

Glossary

atom bomb: a weapon in which the explosive energy is obtained (a) from the breakdown (fission) of atoms of uranium or plutonium into atoms of elements of lighter atomic mass, or, (b) by the fusion of atoms of hydrogen into atoms of helium. The explosive effect of an atom bomb is compared to the explosive force of so many tons of ordinary explosive.

atomic mass: the ratio of the average mass of atoms of an element to $\frac{1}{12}$ of the mass of an atom of carbon 12.

Celsius: (a) Anders Celsius (1701-44), Swedish scientist;
(b) Celsius devised a scale of temperature in which the temperature between the freezing point and the boiling point of water was divided into 100 units. (There are two scales of temperature used in science: the Celsius scale and the Kelvin scale. The freezing point of water is 0°C or 273.15K; the boiling point of water is 100°C or 373.15K at 760 mm mercury air pressure.)

dendrochronology: the study relating the annual ring growth of trees to the date when they were growing.

electrical conductivity: the measurement of the ease with which an electrical current will pass through a substance.

elements: (a) Before the 19th century the elements were regarded as Water, Air, Earth and Fire;
(b) In science since the 18th century "the elements" means substances that cannot be split up by chemical means into atoms of simpler substances.

fossils: remains or traces of past life preserved in rocks.

homo sapiens: a rather vague term, often used to mean modern man.

Kelvin: (a) Lord Kelvin (1824-1907), British scientist;
(b) S.I. unit of temperature equal to one degree Centigrade.

latent heat of evaporation/vaporization: the amount of heat required to convert one kilogram of water to water vapour without rise or fall of temperature. It is measured in joules per kilogram.

manometer: an instrument used to measure the pressure of gases.

nuclei: (a) Small particles around which crystals or droplets of liquid are formed;
(b) Centre portions of atoms in which the mass of the atom is concentrated.

radioactivity: The nuclei of some atoms can break up into smaller portions. This disintegration takes place naturally. At the same time various particles and/or gamma rays are emitted.

Sahel: the land immediately to the south of the Sahara desert. It stretches from Senegal in the west to Somalia in the east of Africa. A number of circumstances, such as population growth, primitive farming methods, cropping natural vegetation for cattle-feed and climate changes, have led to the spread of the desert and to widespread famine.

stratiform: (a) means layer-like; (b) unbroken layers of cloud.

thermal flywheel: A mechanical flywheel stores energy and resists changes of speed, that is, it is difficult to speed it up or slow it down. A thermal flywheel stores thermal heat energy and resists attempts to warm it up or cool it down. A large mass of water can act as a thermal flywheel, hence lands by the sea have more moderate climates than those inside a continent.

Titans: in Greek mythology the sons and daughters of Uranus and Gaea. They fought a long and terrible war with Zeus during which much of the world was devastated.

Book List

Blumenstock, David I., *The Oceans of Air*, Macdonald, 1976
Calder, Nigel, *The Weather Machine*, BBC, 1974
Calder, Nigel, *Timescale*, Chatto and Windus, 1984
Chandler, T.J., *Modern Meteorology and Climatology*, Nelson, 1972
Crisp, Tony, *Weather*, Nelson, 1981
Hanwell, James, *Atmospheric Processes*, Allen and Unwin, 1980
Holford, Ingrid, *The Guinness Book of Weather Facts and Feats*, Book Club Associates, 1978
Humphrey, W.J., and Bentley, W., *Snow Crystals*, Dover Publications, 1931
Pedgley, D.E., *Elementary Meteorology*, HMSO
Wallington, C.E., and Pedgley, D.E., *Know the Weather*, E.P. Publishing Ltd, 1973
Whipple, A.B.C., *Storm*, Time Life, 1982
Wright, Daniel, *Meteorology*, Basil Blackwell, 1983
Young, Eric, *Weather in Britain*, Edward Arnold, 1967
Young, Louise, B., *Earth's Aura*, Allen Lane, 1980

Index